Ly-Lan and the New Class Mix-Up

COMING SOON iN THE
LY-LAN FiNDS A WAY SERIES

Ly-Lan and the Unfair Book Fair

Ly-Lan and the Missing Tooth Fairy

Ly-Lan and the New Class Mix-Up

HÀ DINH

ZONDERkidz™

ZONDERKIDZ

Ly-Lan and the New Class Mix-Up

Copyright © 2025 Hà Dinh
Illustrations © 2025 Hà Dinh

Zonderkidz, 3950 Sparks Drive SE, Suite 101, Grand Rapids, Michigan 49546

Published in Grand Rapids, Michigan, by Zonderkidz. Zonderkidz is a registered
trademark of The Zondervan Corporation, L.L.C., a wholly owned subsidiary of
HarperCollins Christian Publishing, Inc.

Requests for information should be addressed to customercare@harpercollins.com.

ISBN 978-0-310-17489-9 (softcover)
ISBN 978-0-310-17493-6 (audio)
ISBN 978-0-310-17491-2 (ebook)

Library of Congress Control Number: 2025932246

Zondervan titles may be purchased in bulk for educational, business, fundraising, or
sales promotional use. For information, please email SpecialMarkets@Zondervan.com.

Editor: Katherine Jacobs
Art direction: Patti Evans
Cover Design: Patti Evans
Illustrated by: Tracy Nishimura Bishop
Interior Design: Kristen Sasamoto

Printed in the United States of America

25 26 27 28 29 CWR 5 4 3 2 1

To my children and students,
who inspire me to write from my heart.

Chapter 1

This is Ly-Lan. She's eight years old and a soon-to-be third grader. She lives with her parents in Grapevine, Texas. Don't let the *y* in her name confuse you. It makes the long e sound, and you say it like *Lee-Lan*.

When Ly-Lan was born, her parents couldn't decide which grandmother to name her after. Her dad's mother is named Ly.

"My mom is strong-willed, sociable, and loves adventures," Ba says. Ba is the Vietnamese word for dad.

"My mom is Lan and she is kindhearted, generous, and brave," Má says. Má is the Vietnamese word for mom. It's sort of like the English word ma, but with an accent mark that faces the sky over the *a*.

"We named you Ly-Lan after both of them because, to us, you're all of those wonderful things," Ba tells Ly-Lan. He always smiles with a big grin when he tells this story.

Ly-Lan loves hearing stories about her grandmothers and life back in Việt Nam. Việt Nam is a country halfway around the world. Má says it's beautiful there, but Ly-Lan has never been.

She loves hearing about the food they cook, the markets they go to, and the peaceful countryside they call home.

It sounds much different than her life in the

city in America with towering buildings, rows of apartments, and buzzing street corners.

Last summer, Ly-Lan's parents had planned a family trip to Việt Nam. Ly-Lan was excited to see her grandmothers in person for the first time. Ba bought her a travel book filled with pictures of Việt Nam. He even wrote simple Vietnamese phrases in a notebook for Ly-Lan to read aloud and practice every day. "Your grandmothers only speak Vietnamese," Ba reminded her.

But then, Ba started a new job. So now, they are not going until next summer.

When she heard the news, Ly-Lan was sad, but also secretly relieved. She doesn't speak Vietnamese as well as she understands it yet.

She still loves reading her travel book, which is what she is doing when Má peeks her head into Ly-Lan's bedroom.

"Are you practicing the Vietnamese phrases that Ba wrote for you?" Má asks.

Ly-Lan quickly closes her travel book.

"Practice makes progress," she adds.

Ly-Lan looks down. "I know, but I feel like all the words just blend together when I say them. They don't sound as beautiful as when you and Ba say them."

"Your grandmothers would be so happy if you could speak Vietnamese to them," Má points out. "Maybe you can practice it with Cece. She's at the front door."

Cece is Ly-Lan's best friend—ever since they were in the same class in kindergarten. Cece has red hair and freckles on her cheeks. She is spunky, likes to talk like a cowgirl, and always wears a smile on her face. She also loves wearing her cowboy boots

everywhere she goes—except when she's inside Ly-Lan's house. She keeps her boots by the front door since Ly-Lan's family doesn't wear shoes in the house.

"Howdy, neighbor!" Cece says as she pops out from behind Má.

"Cece!!! Perfect timing! Má, I promise I will get back to practicing, but Cece and I have lots to talk about!" Ly-Lan exclaims.

"Like what?" Cece asks with her head tilted.

"Like really important third-grade stuff," Ly-Lan says as she pulls Cece into her room and closes the door.

Ly-Lan knows that Má is right about practicing, but she only needs to speak English at school.

And school is where she is going to tomorrow.

Chapter 2

Ly-Lan is finally going to be a third grader and there are lots of plans and choices to make!

Third grade is where big kids sit at big desks, in big chairs, and read big books. Plus, she heard that third graders can sit anywhere in the cafeteria.

This is going to be the best year yet. I have so many choices to make, Ly-Lan thinks.

Since kindergarten, teachers have told her where to sit.

Now she gets to choose. This is huge. So huge that she and Cece are celebrating by making a plan!

Ly-Lan holds up a hand-drawn map of the cafeteria.

"Look at this, Cece. We can sit anywhere,

with anyone," Ly-Lan says as they sit on the floor of her bedroom.

"Yes! I can smell the cafeteria from here," Cece says.

"Like the smell of the rotten bananas Jimmy McClain left in his lunch box for three days?" Ly-Lan asks.

Jimmy McClain is one of their classmates. He has been in all of her classes since kindergarten too.

"Well, not exactly the rotten bananas! I'm thinking more of the smell of the fresh rolls from the cafeteria ladies," Cece says as she closes her eyes and sniffs, pretending to smell the rolls.

Ly-Lan grabs her notebook and jots down their plans for lunch.

On Mondays, sit closest to the door so it's easy to line up.
On Tuesdays, sit by the wall so we can see the entire cafeteria.

On Wednesdays and Thursdays, sit in the
   middle of the cafeteria so we can hear
   everyone's conversations.
Fridays—FREE CHOICE!

"You know what would make it even
better?" Ly-Lan asks Cece.

"What?" Cece responds.

"If we are in the same class again this year."

"That would be so AMAZINGGG!!! How
did we ever get so lucky all of these years?"
Cece asks.

"Well, you can actually thank me for it," Ly-
Lan brags a little as she twirls her hair.

"What do you mean?" Cece asks.

Ly-Lan looks up at the little wooden cross
hanging in her bedroom. "Every time I need
something, Ba tells me to get on my knees."

Cece nods like she understands. "To beg?
I do that all the time too, especially for extra
ice cream."

"Not beg! To pray!" Ly-Lan exclaims.

Ly-Lan prays with her family every night before bedtime.

Then just like her parents taught her, she walks over to the cross, kneels down, clasps her hands together, closes her eyes, and says a prayer in silence.

"Okay, it's done," Ly-Lan says.

"What did you just do?" Cece asks, tipping her head to the side.

"I prayed to Jesus. My dad says that whenever I need help or have a special wish, I can ask Jesus for it. Every year since kindergarten I have prayed for us to be together. And look, it worked," Ly-Lan points out.

"Oh! That's cool. If I ever need something, I

just yell it across the house and hope that one of my parents gets it for me . . . like, 'Mom, can you ask Principal Grant to have Ly-Lan and me be in the same class again?'"

The girls erupt in giggles.

"So what do we do now?" Cece asks.

"Now we just have to wait and see. That's how prayers work."

Chapter 3

On the first day of school, Ly-Lan brushes her teeth, puts on her new clothes, and heads for the kitchen.

"*Chào*, Má!" Ly-Lan says. *Chào* means hello in Vietnamese.

"Are you excited for third grade?" Má asks with a smile.

"Yes, super! I get to choose my own seat at

lunch, and Cece and I will be in the same class
again."

"How do you know that, *bé*?" Má asks, as
she makes Ly-Lan's lunch.

Ly-Lan makes a face. "Don't call me *bé*, Má.
I'm not a 'little one' anymore—I'm older now!
And I prayed for Cece and me to be in the
same classroom again. That's how I know it
will happen."

"I'm not sure that's how prayers work, Ly-Lan. But I hope you will be with her again," Má says as she combs through Ly-Lan's hair with her fingers. Then she places her lunch box on the table. "I packed your favorite seedless grapes."

"If they don't have seeds inside, are they still a fruit?" Ly-Lan wonders.

"Good question. They are definitely not what you expect from a fruit," Má says.

"Nope! They're better!" Ly-Lan says, grinning.

Ly-Lan slurps down her cereal and jets off to the bus stop.

Mr. Clark opens the door of the bus. He used to be a truck driver. Now he's a bus driver who wears glasses and a trucker hat and always greets everyone by name, with a warm and inviting smile.

"Good morning, Mr. Clark!" Ly-Lan says.

"Good morning, Ly-Lan!" says Mr. Clark. "So glad to see you again."

"Same here! It's going to be the BEST YEAR EVER!"

She rushes to her seat where Cece is already waiting for her.

"Are you ready, BFF?!" Ly-Lan asks.

"I was born ready," Cece says and gives Ly-Lan a big hug.

The bus fills up quickly with familiar faces and voices. But at the next stop, a new girl with long black hair gets on the bus. She looks like a picture in Ly-Lan's travel book.

"Who's that?" Ly-Lan whispers to Cece.

"Looks like a new student," Cece predicts.

Ly-Lan stands up to get a better look, but the bus jolts and she falls forward.

"Are you OK?" Cece asks.

"Yes, I'm fine." Ly-Lan smiles and sits back down.

Jimmy McClain's head pops up from the seat behind them. "What are you up to?"

Jimmy McClain is one of the smartest kids at school. He is also one of the most curious kids Ly-Lan knows. He seems to know about everything. And loves to know what everyone around him is doing.

"Oh, hey Jimmy," Ly-Lan says, turning to him.

"Looking over our plans for lunch," Cece answers.

"What do you mean?" Jimmy asks.

"Don't you know that third graders can sit anywhere in the cafeteria? Maybe one day we want to sit at the front table with all of our

friends; maybe we want to sit alone in the back; or maybe we want to sit at the same table every day. We can finally choose where to sit and who to sit with! We can make our own choices!" Ly-Lan says loudly.

"Who cares? Lunch is only thirty minutes long. Or should I say thirty minutes short? If you think about it, it takes five minutes to walk to the cafeteria, five minutes to get all your food out and ready, 15 minutes to eat, and then five minutes to clean up. It's not even enough time to finish my food," Jimmy complains.

"Is that why you left the banana in your lunch box for three whole days last year?" Cece jokes.

The bus explodes into laughter. Some kids laugh so hard they snort!

Jimmy's face turns red with embarrassment. "Hey! That's not funny. It was an accident and exactly my point! I didn't have enough time to finish it. So I kept it in my lunch box and never had enough time to eat it. That's how it went bad."

"You do have a point, Jimmy! We really don't have enough time. That's why it's important for us to have a plan!" Ly-Lan says, pointing her index finger to the sky to make her point.

Jimmy grins because he loves it when he hears he's right. He sits back down and hides inside a chapter book.

Cece looks at the new girl then turns to Ly- Lan. "I know you're wondering who that new girl is and if she'll be in our class."

Cece always seems to know when Ly-Lan has something on her mind.

"I'm more worried if I'll be in the same class with you," Ly-Lan says, looking at Cece. "Did you ask your mom to call the principal?"

"What? I thought you said praying was enough?" Cece responds.

They look at each other with the biggest eyes as the bus comes to a screeching stop at the front of school.

Chapter 4

Good morning, boys and girls!" Principal Grant says. She stands by the door of the school each morning.

Principal Grant is in charge of Canyon Ridge View Elementary School. She has short, blond hair and clickety heels that you can hear from down the hall.

"Hi, Principal Grant!" Ly-Lan greets her.

"Welcome back! Are you excited to be in third grade this year?" she asks.

"It's funny you ask! We have something important to ask you, Partner. Just kidding, I mean Principal Grant," Cece says. "Are we in the same class? Are we? Are we?"

"And if we're not, can you make the change now?" Ly-Lan asks as she raises her eyebrows and looks up.

Principal Grant gives a big belly laugh, the kind that parents do before they tell kids no. "Well, the class lists are posted on the teachers' doors," she says.

Ly-Lan and Cece dash up the stairs and down to the third-grade hallway.

"Walking feet only,"

Principal Grant calls out loudly from behind them.

Ly-Lan rushes to the door to her right. Cece sprints to the door to the left.

They both find the lists of names and scan them from top to the bottom with their index finger.

The hallway fills up quickly with children and chatter in every corner.

Standing at opposite classroom doors, the girls turn to stare at each other in shock.

"You're in this class," Cece says, pointing to the classroom in front of her.

"And you're in this one," Ly-Lan says as she points to the classroom in front of her. Her jaw drops and her eyes begin swelling up with tears.

The bell rings and children rush back and forth in the hallways to begin finding their names too.

"Hi there, Cece," Miss Garcia says. "So glad you're with me this year!"

"Oh, hi Miss Garcia," Cece stutters.

Miss Garcia takes Cece's hand and leads her into the room.

Cece follows Miss Garcia in silence as she looks back at Ly-Lan, still frozen in the hallway.

So that's it? We're just going to go our separate ways? Ly-Lan thinks to herself.

She turns and looks into her new classroom with teary eyes.

"No. No way. I'm just going to stand here until my name is on Miss Garcia's list. Ba says that I'm strong-willed like Grandma Ly, so I'm not going in there," Ly-Lan mutters under her breath.

Just then Mr. H walks over to her. Mr. H is short for Mr. Hargesheimer.

"Good morning, young lady," Mr. H says to Ly-Lan.

"Hi, Mr. H," Ly-Lan answers.

Mr. H is a tall man with an unusually deep and calming voice.

"I have a seat right here in the front row for you." Mr. H points to the front of the room.

"Actually, I need you to write my name on Miss Garcia's list," Ly-Lan says and points at the roster on the door across the hall.

Looking confused, Mr. H asks, "Why would I do that? You're on my class list."

Ly-Lan explains that she and Cece had been in the same classroom since kindergarten and they have been great students together. Why change it now when it's best for them to be together?

"Students don't get to choose their class, Ly-Lan. My seating chart says you belong right here," Mr. H says, holding up his seating chart. "Please, come in before the tardy bell rings or I will have to mark you tardy."

Ly-Lan sighs, drops her shoulders, and drags herself to her seat in Mr. H's third-grade classroom.

Somehow her new big desk and big chair don't feel so impressive now.

She plops her backpack down on the floor next to her chair and places both elbows on the desktop, her hands covering her face.

RINGGGGG! RINGGGGG!

Ly-Lan jumps. "Ahhhhh!"

"It's just the tardy bell," says a familiar voice from behind her.

Ly-Lan turns around and sees none other than Jimmy.

"Ugh, Jimmy," she moans.

"Oh, aren't you excited that we're in the same class?" Jimmy asks.

Jimmy always seems to be wherever Ly-Lan is—on the school bus, in the cafeteria, and now in her class *again*.

Why is Jimmy here and not Cece? Did I say

the wrong name when I was praying? Ly-Lan wonders.

Just then, the new girl from the school bus walks in with Principal Grant.

"Hi, class! This is Quyên Lê. She's a new student at our school. She speaks Vietnamese but is learning English. Please make her feel welcome!" Principal Grant has a hand on her shoulder.

"My cousin has the same name, Quinn," Jimmy announces to the class.

Mr. H smiles and points to the chair next to Ly-Lan. "Hi, Quyên! I'm Mr. H and this is Ly- Lan. You'll be sitting right here."

Then he turns to Ly-Lan and says, "Do you mind helping Quyên out as she adjusts to our school and classroom?"

Ly-Lan is one of the few students who knows enough Vietnamese to help new Vietnamese students at school, and she is usually good about helping.

Má says that Ly-Lan is generous like Grandma Lan. Generous means helping others even when you're not expected to.

Two years ago, she helped the Phạm twins when they were new to Canyon Ridge View and even played with them at recess. But now? Ly-Lan can't help but think about her best friend in Miss Garcia's class.

Quyên looks at Ly-Lan and smiles at her,

but Ly-Lan can't get herself to smile back. She just stares at the front board as Mr. H introduces himself and goes over the schedule for third grade.

Chapter 5

Beep! *Beep! Beep!* The alarm on Mr. H's watch buzzes.

"It's lunchtime! Let's line up. I will tell you where you'll be sitting this year," Mr. H says.

"Tell us where we'll be sitting this year?" Ly-Lan repeats. "I thought third graders could sit anywhere we want?"

"The rules have changed," Mr. H tells the class.

Ly-Lan's shoulders droop again.

"Last year many kids were so rowdy at lunch that Mrs. Grant decided to go back to assigned seats this year," Mr. H continues.

Oh no! I already made plans with Cece, Ly-Lan thinks.

"Can we not choose where to sit? I thought third graders have more choices," Ly-Lan points out.

"You do have many choices in third grade. One of them is choosing to be really good friends with the kids at your table. I'm sure you'll end up being best friends by the end of the year," Mr. H says as he pats Ly-Lan's back.

"You mean we have to sit in the same seat all year?" Ly-Lan says.

Adults choose everything for kids—whose class we're in, where we sit at lunch, and who we sit with! she almost yells in her head.

As she gets in line, Ly-Lan crosses her arms and whispers under her breath, "Today is officially the worst first day ever."

The rest of the class begins lining up and Quyên quickly takes her place behind Ly-Lan.

The line slowly moves out of the classroom and down the hallway.

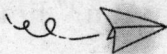

The cafeteria looks the same as it did last year with rows of long tables and chairs that squeak every time someone moves.

Mr. H points to a seat and Ly-Lan drops herself into the chair and swings her lunch box on top of the table.

"Quyên, you can sit here next to Ly-Lan and Jimmy," Mr. H says.

Ly-Lan stares at Quyên and then down at her lunch box.

Just then, Cece's class walks into the cafeteria. Ly-Lan watches Cece sit down at a long table on the other side of the cafeteria. Her face feels warm as tears fall down her cheeks.

"Are you OK, Ly-Lan?" Jimmy asks quietly.

"Yeah, I guess. It's just one of those days. I don't really want to talk about it," Ly-Lan replies.

Just then, Quyên takes a napkin from her lunch box and hands it Ly-Lan.

Ly-Lan smiles a little at Quyên, then wipes off her tears.

She opens her lunch box but none of the food looks good. She slurps her juice box and sits in silence the rest of lunchtime. Ly-Lan doesn't touch the seedless grapes. Not even her favorite fruit can cheer her up.

The rest of the day is a blur and then the afternoon dismissal bell rings.

"Hey, young lady!" Mr. Clark says to Ly-Lan as she climbs onto the bus.

Ly-Lan waves and cracks a small smile at

Mr. Clark—so small that Mr. Clark cannot even see it.

"Are you OK?" Mr. Clark asks.

"Well, I was supposed to be in the same class as Cece, but I'm not," Ly-Lan shares.

"So is it a mix-up?"

"Mix-up? Like a mistake?"

"You said you two are *supposed* to be together. So maybe someone made a mistake and put you in the wrong class?"

Ly-Lan eyes grow wide.

"Maybe so, maybe it is a mix-up," she says slowly as she takes her seat next to Cece.

"Cece, do you think it was a mix-up?" Ly- Lan asks.

"Like someone messed up the class lists? But who? Who? Who? We need to find that person," Cece insists.

"No. I think we already know who they are. Who makes all the big decisions around here?" Ly-Lan asks her friend.

"Mr. Clark!" Cece shouts out.

"No, Cece! Not on this bus! I mean for the entire school!" Ly-Lan responds just as loudly.

"Ohhhh . . . I see where you're going with this," Cece says. "Actually, just kidding. Where are you going with this?"

"I may have to go straight to the principal's office for this one, Cece," Ly-Lan remarks as she squints her eyes and points in the direction of the school, which also happens to be in the same direction Quyên is as she is taking a seat on the bus.

"Oops! Sorry! I'm not pointing at you," Ly-Lan quickly says to Quyên as she pulls her hand back and covers her face.

Quyên smiles and settles into the seat across the aisle.

Chapter 6

"How was your first day?" Má asks Ly-Lan at the dinner table. She places stir-fried green beans with beef, rice, and squash soup in the middle of the table.

"I'm glad you asked. It was the worst day ever!" Ly-Lan groans, grabbing her chopsticks and a small bowl of rice.

"I could tell something was wrong." Má nods. "You didn't even eat your favorite grapes."

"What happened?" Ba asks Ly-Lan.

"Well, I prayed for Cece and me to be in the same class again. You said that if I really want something, I should pray for it. So I did. I even got on my knees to pray. That's how much I really wanted it. But guess what? My prayer was not answered and my wish was not granted. Plus, there's a new girl at school from Việt Nam and I have to help her," Ly-Lan says in a rush, covering her face with both hands.

"That sounds like a very eventful day!" Ba says.

Má adds, "And a very emotional day as well."

"Now can you say it again in Vietnamese?" Ba encourages Ly-Lan.

"Dad!!! Not now. Ughhh . . ." Ly-Lan sighs.

"I'm sorry you and Cece aren't in the same class, but things don't always work out the way we want them to, even if we pray for it," Ba says.

"And God isn't a genie, Ly-Lan. He doesn't just grant us wishes." Má takes a spoonful of soup.

"Then why did you teach me how to pray, if prayers aren't always answered?" Ly-Lan asks her parents.

"Prayers are like wishes from our hearts, but sometimes our wishes aren't always the best thing for us. Only God can decide that. We have to trust Him," Má says.

"Trust?" Ly-Lan says. "I trusted that Cece and I were going to be in the same class. I trusted that we got to choose our own seats at lunch. I trusted that my prayers would be answered. I trusted, and look what happened."

"I know you've had a lot of disappointments today, but you can't have your way all the time, Ly-Lan," Má says.

"You have to trust that God knows what's best, even if you don't see it now. Maybe this is your opportunity to practice speaking Vietnamese with the new student? What's her name?" Ba wants Ly-Lan to see the good in what is happening.

"Her name is Quyên. And I'm not asking for everything to go my way all the time. Just sometimes—especially now would be great," Ly-Lan mutters.

Ba walks over and rubs Ly-Lan's head, then gently squeezes her shoulders.

"I don't really think this was all a mistake, Ly-Lan. I think you should use this opportunity to make new friends," Má suggests.

"If praying is not going to help and God doesn't grant wishes, I'm going to take my chances on someone at school who can grant me my wish," Ly-Lan says as she eats her squash soup with rice.

"What do you mean? Are you thinking about Principal Grant? She's not a genie, Ly-Lan. She doesn't grant wishes either," Ba insists with a big belly laugh.

"Oh, Ba. You just watch. I'll find a way," Ly-Lan says with a little smirk.

After dinner, Ly-Lan heads to her room. She writes in her notebook.

Dear Principal Grant,
    It's me, Ly-Lan Trần.
    Cece Campbell and I have been best friends since kindergarten and there has been a "mix-up," like a mistake. I'm in Mr. H's class and she's in Miss Garcia's.
    No need to say sorry. Mix-ups happen. I get it, and both teachers are pretty good, but please put us together again.

My mom says you're a principal and not a genie so you don't grant wishes, but do you know it's actually in your name? G-R-A-N-T! It's literally in your name! So please. Please. I'm begging. We are very good students together.

You're a real
PAL, Princi-PAL!
Ly-Lan Trần

Ly-Lan tears the letter from her notebook and puts it in her backpack.

Chapter 7

The next morning, as Principal Grant greets students at the front doors, Ly-Lan slips the letter into her hands and dashes to class.

She hurries through the door, waving and smiling to everyone.

"Why are you so happy today?" Jimmy whispers in Ly-Lan's ear as she sits down.

"What do you mean?" She raises her eyebrows so high, her forehead wrinkles.

"You were super sad yesterday and now you're so happy. Do you have something up your sleeve?" Jimmy asks.

"Up my sleeve? I don't even have sleeves on today. See?" Ly-Lan says as she holds out both of her arms.

"No, I mean you look like you have something planned but you're not telling anyone," Jimmy says.

"Well, I have a feeling Cece and I will be in the same class again."

Just then Ly-Lan hears the clicky-clackity sound of high heels walking down the hallway.

Principal Grant peeks in.

"Can I see Ly-Lan in the hallway for a second?" she asks Mr. H.

The entire class gasps as if Ly-Lan is in trouble—and it's only the second day of school.

"This is what I'm talking about, Jimmy. You just watch," Ly-Lan says, her head held high.

In the hallway, Principal Grant kneels down next to Ly-Lan. She has the letter in her hand.

"I know you've been in the same class with Cece for a long time, Ly-Lan, but this is a chance for you to make new friends this year," she explains.

"But we really want to be in the same class together," Ly-Lan pleads.

"That's just not how it works, Ly-Lan. Make new friends with other kids like Quyên. You'll still get to play with Cece at recess. As a matter of fact, you can introduce her to Quyên and you can all be best friends together," Principal Grant suggests.

"All be best friends together? I've always had just one best friend and it's Cece and it's been Cece since kindergarten. I don't think you understand, Principal Grant. This is all a mix-up," Ly-Lan says.

"Why don't you take this opportunity to get to know Quyên better? You might just find a best friend in her too? And by the way, thank you for making her feel welcomed at our school. You've always been such a great friend," Principal Grant says as she pats Ly-Lan on the back and motions her to go back to class.

Patting kids on their backs is another thing that adults like Ba and Má do before they tell kids no. Ly-Lan knows this all too well.

Ly-Lan walks back into the classroom feeling like a balloon without air.

She sinks down into the big kid chair she used to be excited about and hides her face.

Just then, she feels a warm hand on her shoulder.

Ly-Lan opens her eyes. Quyên is smiling at her.

Quyên's smile instantly makes Ly-Lan think of Principal Grant's last words to her.

"Me? A good friend? Am I really?" Ly-Lan mutters under her breath.

"Are you okay?" Jimmy says.

"What do you mean?" Ly-Lan looks over her shoulder at Jimmy.

"According to your facial expressions and body language, you are showing signs of sadness and disappointment," Jimmy says.

"Where do you even get these words, Jimmy? I'm fine. Just forget what I said about switching classes. I changed my mind."

Prayers don't work. Writing letters doesn't work. What is there left to do? Ly-Lan sighs.

What if I make new friends and Cece makes new friends? Will we still be best friends or will she have another best friend?

She looks out the window as Mr. H explains about conducting science experiments.

"Sometimes scientists are not successful on their own," he says. "When that happens, they reach out to other scientists for help."

Help? If prayers don't work and wishes aren't granted, then who can help me find another way? Má! Má! Ly-Lan thinks to herself.

But after their talk last night, Ly-Lan isn't sure if Má feels the same way she does.

The alarm on Mr. H's watch beeps. Lunchtime.

"Guess we'll pick this lesson back up after lunch, class," Mr. H says.

Everyone quickly lines up.

Ly-Lan grabs her lunch box. Quyên gets in line behind her.

As Ly-Lan takes her seat in the cafeteria next to Quyên, Cece walks in with her class, giggling with some of her classmates. Cece waves at Ly-Lan. Ly-Lan waves back. Cece then takes a seat and begins talking and laughing with her new friends.

Ly-Lan looks down at her lunch box and closes her eyes.

Even with her eyes shut, she can still see Cece having fun with her new friends. The more she thinks about it, the warmer her face becomes and the more disappointed she feels.

Chapter 8

After school, Ly-Lan takes her seat on the bus and puts her backpack where Cece usually sits.

"Ly-Lan, can you move your backpack, please?" Cece asks, standing next to her.

"No. Not today. You can sit with your new best friends from the cafeteria," Ly-Lan says.

Cece furrows her eyebrows, making wrinkles on her forehead. "What do you mean?" Cece asks.

"You don't seem to care that we're not in the same class. I'm the only one who's sad and upset about it. I'm the only one who wrote a letter to Principal Grant," Ly-Lan says, holding back tears.

"You didn't tell me that you were writing to Principal Grant, and I do care. But what can I do about it? I'm not a teacher or the principal. And you can make new friends in your class too!" Cece points out.

"You sound just like my parents and Principal Grant!" Ly-Lan whines a little. "I know I can make new friends. I just wish we were in the same class again, but it sounds like you don't even care."

"I do, but I can't change it. You can't either," Cece responds.

"In that case, maybe the new girl will be my best friend and you won't," Ly-Lan shouts.

Ly-Lan knows the moment those words leave her lips that they aren't true. But they

have already been said, and she can't take them back.

"Take it back," Cece insists.

"Take what back?" Ly-Lan pretends to be confused.

"Your mean words. You don't mean them," Cece says.

But Ly-Lan doesn't know how to stop.

"You don't care that we're not in the same class anymore. I saw you at lunch having a good time without me."

"What do you want me to do, Ly-Lan?" Cece asks.

"Nothing," Ly-Lan murmurs and looks away.

Cece walks to the back of the bus with tears in her eyes.

Ly-Lan never sat on the bus without Cece before.

She feels extra lonely without her best friend. She's mad and sad all mixed together.

The bus finally stops at Ly-Lan's street, and she walks to the front with her shoulders slumped.

"What's wrong, Ly-Lan?" asks Mr. Clark.

"Cece's making new best friends in her classroom when I'm supposed to be her best friend," Ly-Lan responds.

Mr. Clark scratches his head. "It's okay to have more than one best friend, Ly-Lan. I have about five best friends."

"You do?" Ly-Lan asks as Mr. Clark nods.

"Yes, my wife, my three kids, and my childhood friend are all my best friends! The more the merrier."

Ly-Lan never thought of having more than one best friend before. She always had Cece, and that was always enough. And she didn't consider her parents being best friends either.

She waves goodbye and slowly walks off the bus and the rest of the way home.

The thought of having more than one best friend at school seems complicated to Ly-Lan. How could she ever divide up her time between two or more best friends? Plus, who would really be *the* best friend if she had more than one? If she added another best friend, would Cece feel jealous? Or worse, what if *she* is the one feeling jealous?

But maybe having more best friends is more fun. Are Ba and Má my best friends too? Maybe more is merrier? wonders Ly-Lan.

Chapter 9

That night for dinner, Má makes Ly-Lan's favorite noodle soup—phở. The aroma of the broth makes Ly-Lan feel warm and peaceful inside.

"Did your day go better today?" Má asks.

"Well, it came and it went," Ly-Lan responds, looking at her phở.

"No, really. How did it go?" chimes in Ba.

"I wrote a letter to Principal Grant last night," Ly-Lan admits.

Má looks at her. "You did? Did you ask her to change your class, Ly-Lan Trần?"

Má only uses her whole name when she's about to get in BIG trouble.

"I asked her very nicely, but she said she wouldn't change the class list, and now Cece is making new best friends. So, I guess it's a win for everyone except me," Ly-Lan says, moving her chopsticks back and forth in her soup.

"But you are still best friends, right?" Má asks.

"Well, I got really upset so I told her that we're not best friends anymore," Ly-Lan confesses, hanging her head.

"Oh, Ly-Lan." Ba hugs her from behind.

"I didn't mean it, Ba. I just want things the way they were before. My prayers went unanswered. Principal Grant won't grant me my wish, which is silly because it's actually in her name to grant wishes. And so from now on, she is Principal Un-Grant to me," Ly-Lan says, still twirling the noodles in her bowl.

Suddenly, Ly-Lan looks up. "But maybe you can help, Má. Today in class Mr. H told us that sometimes scientists need help with their experiments and they reach out to other scientists. Maybe you can help me out and work your magic, Má. I think principals will listen to parents more than kids."

"What special magic do you think I have, Ly-Lan?" asks Má.

"The kind of magic that makes food so delicious, like this bowl of noodles."

Má gives a big belly laugh—the kind of laugh that Ly-Lan knows is followed by a no.

"I think we all know that Principal Grant's decision is the final decision. We just have to accept that and make the best out of this situation," Má says.

"Everyone keeps telling me no," Ly-Lan says. "But I've found a way to make it work. Everyone just has to agree with it."

Ba smiles. "Sometimes our anger gets the best of us when we don't get our way. Remember when we had to cancel our trip to Việt Nam? You were disappointed, but it's given you more time to learn Vietnamese, which I am still very happy to practice with you whenever you want to."

"Ba, not now," Ly-Lan groans.

"You're definitely strong-willed like *bà nội*, Ba's mom, Ly-Lan," Má says. "But you're also very kindhearted too like *bà ngoại*, my mom, remember?"

Ba squeezes Ly-Lan's hand. "Why don't you use this opportunity to be friends with Quyên?

She might even be another best friend to you one day."

"Do you mean to say the more the merrier?" Ly-Lan asks. "That's what Mr. Clark said to me on the bus today."

Ba answers, "Right! Take this chance to make more new friends. The more the merrier, like Mr. Clark said."

"You don't just have one grandma, you have two! You don't just have one first name, you have two! See? The more the merrier," Má insists.

Ly-Lan thinks about Má's words. They all make sense, but it's hard to admit that she's been wrong this entire time.

This growing up business is no fun. Can I just close my eyes and go back to second grade, when life was easier? Ly-Lan wonders as she finishes her soup.

Chapter 10

After dinner, Ly-Lan zooms straight into her
bedroom.

She lies on her bed, with her hands behind
her head, and stares up at the ceiling.

*I prayed for my best friend to be in my
class, but that didn't come true. What is the
point of praying if it doesn't come true?* Ly-Lan
thinks.

Then she remembers how Cece was in

her room just the other day and how happy they were.

Have I been a good friend to Cece?

Sure, they aren't in the same classroom anymore and that is frustrating, but she made it much worse by taking it out on her very best friend.

Ly-Lan imagines making new friends like Cece.

Could I even make another best friend—like Quyên?

The idea of having more friends and getting to know Quyên better doesn't seem so bad anymore. It even seems a little bit exciting.

Ly-Lan takes out her travel book and turns to the page with the girls sitting under the palm trees.

I wonder if Quyên eats the same food that I eat at home. I wonder if she has gone to the markets that both of my grandmas have gone to? Has she seen the peaceful countryside in Việt Nam too?

Ly-Lan gets out her notebook and turns to a clean page. She begins to write:

1. Practice more Vietnamese
2. Make a new friend or two
3. Make up with Cece

But first, write an apology to Cece.

She turns the page to write a letter to Cece, but then closes the notebook. She opens it again, stares at the lines, then closes it up again.

There's nothing easier to do than write a

note to my best friend. I've done it a million times, Ly-Lan thinks.

But there's also nothing harder to do than admit you have been wrong.

I have to do this.

When she opens up the notebook again, it goes to the page with the cafeteria seating plans that she made with Cece.

How excited they were making it together, and how happy they were as friends!

It doesn't really matter where we sit in the cafeteria or what class we're in, Cece will always be my best friend, Ly-Lan finally admits to herself.

Ly-Lan picks up a crayon and writes *Ly-Lan + Cece = BFFs* in the middle of the plans and draws a heart around it. She tears the page from the notebook and places it in her backpack.

"I will give this to Cece tomorrow and explain everything," she says out loud.

Tomorrow, I need to make so many things right.

Ly-Lan's bedroom door creaks open.

"Ly-Lan, we wanted to check on you," Ba says as he and Má slip through the door and sit on the corner of her bed.

"I feel horrible about the way I treated Cece, but I will make it up to her tomorrow," Ly-Lan promises.

Má nods. "People make mistakes all the time, Ly-Lan. The most important thing is for you to learn from them and ask for forgiveness."

Ly-Lan nods and puts her head on Má's lap.

Má then asks, "Remember when you asked me if grapes are considered a fruit if they don't have seeds? What did you say after that?"

"I said that they were better," Ly-Lan replies.

"Because they're not what you expected grapes to be, they're better. That's how life can be sometimes, Ly-Lan. Maybe third grade isn't what you expected it to be," Má says.

"But maybe it's better," Ly-Lan adds as she looks up at Má and smiles.

Ba smiles too. "Good job, bé!"

"Ba, I'm not a little girl anymore, you know," Ly-Lan insists.

"No, you are a big third grader! Now, are you ready for prayers?" Ba asks.

"Yes," Ly-Lan says. She bows her head. "Dear God, bless my family. And please help me to be a better friend. Amen."

"Amen," say Má and Ba.

Chapter 11

The next day, Ly-Lan sees Cece on the bus.

"Can I sit next to you?" Ly-Lan asks.

Cece replies, "If you want to."

"This is for you," Ly-Lan says as she slips the paper into Cece's hand.

Cece unfolds it and looks at the plans with their names and the big heart added. She smiles.

"I'm sorry. I was really mad, and I took it out on you," Ly-Lan says in a rush.

"If I could, I would have us in the same classroom again. You know I would," Cece says.

"I was really upset, and it wasn't your fault."

"It's no one's fault, really. Just promise me we'll always be best friends?" Cece asks.

Ly-Lan can hardly believe it. Cece forgives her, even after all the mean things she said to her. Cece is still her best friend!

"Promise! See? It says so on the paper," Ly-Lan says as Cece pulls her in for a hug.

Just then, Jimmy pops up behind them. "I knew something was going on with the two of you yesterday."

"Oh, Jimmy! You just know all the things, don't you?" Ly-Lan says with a smile.

Ly-Lan looks up at the big rearview mirror in front of the bus. She sees Mr. Clark smiling back at her.

When the bus stops at school, Ly-Lan and Cece walk together to the third-grade hallway.

It feels like it was before. They are still best friends in third grade, even if they are in different classrooms.

At lunch, Ly-Lan sees Cece sitting with her new friends across the cafeteria.

She waves to her and then takes her seat next to Quyên.

"Big," Quyên says in English, pointing to Ly-Lan's grapes.

Ly-Lan's eyes grow wide. She can't believe Quyên just spoke and even said an English word!

Ly-Lan exclaims, "Yes, big! They are big!"

"*Bự*," Quyên says and points to the grapes again.

"Yes! I know what that means. *Bự* means big in Vietnamese," Ly-Lan says proudly.

Quyên points to the grapes. "*Nho.*"

"No?" Jimmy asks.

"No, Jimmy. She said *nho* and you say it like *nyaw*," Ly-Lan explains.

"What does that mean?"

"It means grapes in Vietnamese," Ly-Lan says with the biggest grin.

"Yes!" Quyên smiles big too.

Ly-Lan wishes that she knew more Vietnamese words to say to Quyên, but maybe Quyên can help her practice.

Ly-Lan spends the rest of lunch sitting in her assigned seat pointing to different things in her lunch box and telling Quyên what they are in English.

Quyên then says them back in Vietnamese. Ly-Lan tries to remember the words to tell Ba and Má after school.

Having assigned seats isn't so bad after all, Ly-Lan decides as she eats her favorite grapes.

She's no longer with her best friend all day at school, but she's making a new one.

She can't choose her own seat for lunch, but she wouldn't trade it for anything else.

Just then Jimmy shouts across the table to Quyên, "Hi! I'm Jimmy McClain. I knew you could speak English!"

The entire table starts to giggle. "Oh, Jimmy! You just know everything, don't you?" Ly-Lan asks.

Later on the school bus, Ly-Lan finds Cece and sits next to her.

"Maybe this class mix-up happened so we all can grow from it," Cece says.

Ly-Lan jumps up from her seat as her jaw drops toward the floor of the bus.

"Wait! You're sounding more like an adult every day, Cece. That's what my mom said to me. How did you know that?"

"I didn't. That's what my mom said to me," Cece says with wide eyes.

"Whoa . . . moms are really magical, huh?" Ly-Lan exclaims.

Just then Quyên gets on the bus. Ly-Lan waves her over.

"Cece, this is Quyên. She's my new friend."

Ly-Lan then points to Cece and says, "Cece."

Quyên smiles and says, "Hello!" and takes the seat next to the girls.

Cece leans forward and says, "*Chào!* HOWDY!"

Ly-Lan and Quyên start giggling.

Cece starts chuckling too.

"Maybe Quyên can teach us more Vietnamese. We can all learn together," Cece whispers to Ly-Lan.

"Together? I like the sound of that," Ly-Lan agrees.

Because why learn Vietnamese alone when

*I can learn it with my best friend and my new
friend? Maybe more is merrier?*

And in that moment, Ly-Lan realizes
that the new class mix-up was not a mix-up
after all.

Glossary

ba: /BAH/ dad

bà ngoại: /bah ngwhy/ maternal grandma
(mom's mom)

bà nội: / bah noy/ paternal grandma
(dad's mom)

bé: /BEH/ little one

bự: /buhg/ big

chào: /chou/ hello

má: /MAH/ mom

phở: /fuh/ a Vietnamese broth soup with meat,
rice noodles, and herbs

nho: /nyaw / grapes

Scan this QR code for a special video by author
Ha Dinh to hear some of the Vietnamese words
that appear in this book pronounced.

Practice saying them out loud along with her!

WATCH FOR
Ly-Lan and the Unfair Book Fair
COMING iN 2026!

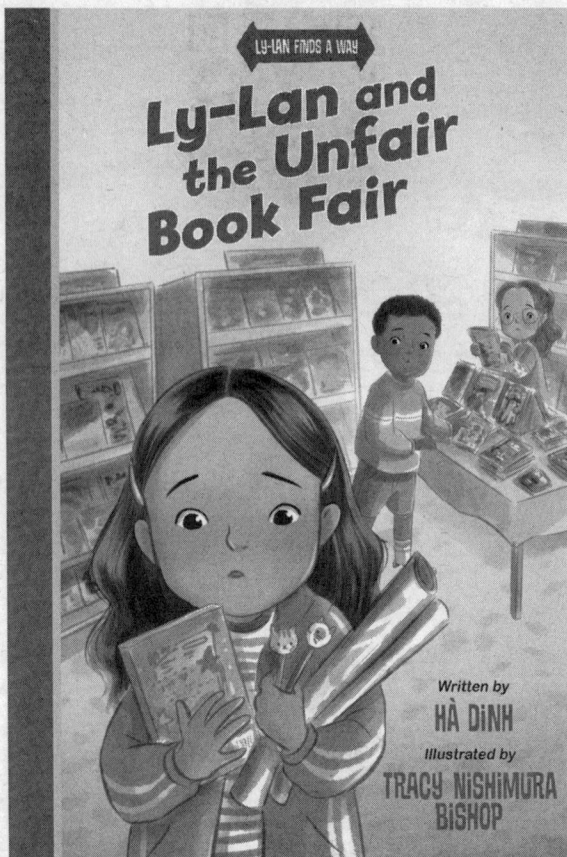